The Little
Yoga

J.P. Vaswani

Compiled and Edited by
Dr. Prabha Sampath
and
Krishna Kumari

New Dawn

NEW DAWN
a division of Sterling Publishers (P) Ltd.
A-59, Okhla Industrial Area, Phase-II, New Delhi-110020.
Tel: 26387070, 26386209; Fax: 91-11-26383788
E-mail: info@sterlingpublishers.com
www.sterlingpublishers.com

The Little Book Of Yoga
© 2003, Sterling Publishers Private Limited
ISBN 81 207 2586 7
Reprint 2004, 2005

Published by Sterling Publishers Pvt. Ltd., New Delhi-110020.
Lasertypeset by Vikas Compographics, New Delhi-110020.
Printed at Sai Early Learners (P) Ltd., New Delhi-110020.

Dedication

*All that is in this book, I learnt at Thy
Lotus Feet, Master! (Sadhu Vaswani)*

To Thee I dedicate this slim volume

- J.P. Vaswani

Contents

Contents

Yoga – For You And Me

Man today stands on a planet of limitless promise. He has entered a new age – the Space Age, as it is called. His rockets have crossed distant planets. He has reached the zenith of technological brilliance. He has probed the secrets of the atom. He has measured the depths of the ocean. He has unravelled the mysteries of his body and mind. And yet - he is still confused as to his own being and the real purpose of his life. He is faced with a terrible loneliness. His heart is stirred by a thousand fears which he cannot name.

Until man is able to conquer his inner nature, his internal nature, can he be said to be any higher than the animals?

The spider can spin along his way. The ant is regarded as the greatest organiser in the world. The monkey can put to shame the most competent trapeze artist. The turtle can exist for over 300 years. Therefore, the measure of man is not just a strong enduring body. The measure of man is not his command over mathematics. The measure of man is not his scientific or artistic capabilities. The measure of man is his control over himself, his lower self, his passions, his pride, his thoughts and aspirations, his dreams and his deeds, his emotions and feelings.

In recent years, in Europe and America, in fact even in India, interest in yoga is increasing. A number of people want to know more and more about yoga. But I am afraid not many know what true yoga is.

Each one of us has seen the wonder of the wonderland. We have beheld the Face Divine. We have heard the magic notes of the melody of the Master's Flute. The Eternal Krishna, the Eternal Christ is within every one of us. But we have forgotten this great truth, and therefore we feel frustrated with life. We feel so weak, so poor, and so desperate. We lack the strength and the energy to face life. We forget that we are inheritors of a rich glory. Within us is a foundation of inspiration. Infinite treasures, energies of the spirit, lie locked up within us. Forgetting these great truths, we run after the shadows of life. We chase shadow shapes of wealth and possessions, pleasure and power. We are busy gathering silver and gold, amassing riches. But we neglect our richest treasure – the treasure that is within us. Unlock this treasure! Unfold this power! And you will find there is nothing that you cannot achieve.

Suppose, I were to tell you, that at a particular spot in the north–east corner of a plot of land, there lies buried a treasure-trove – pots of silver and gold, rubies and diamonds; I am sure many of you would start digging and digging into the earth. You would forsake your food and sleep; you would forsake your kith and kin. You would keep on digging until you find the treasure-trove.

And yet, a treasure richer by far than all the wealth of the world, lies hidden within you. And you do nothing to discover it. The way to discover it is the way of yoga.

There are so many people today, who do not know what true yoga is. They confound yoga with the occult. They think that a yogi is a man with a long flowing beard, with large, red eyes. They feel that the yogi is a man whose body is smeared with ashes; who lives in a cave and subsists on the barks of trees. They imagine that the yogi is a man who can fly in the air, walk on the waters, pass through a fire and come out unscathed. A person who can drink poison, and not be affected by it; a person who can materialise things out of thin air, someone who can convert base metals into gold.

Yoga is *not* magic. And the true yogi is *not* a magician. He is *not* a wonder worker or a miracle man. A true yogi is a man of wisdom.

What Is Yoga?

The word yoga is derived from the Sanskrit word *yug* – which means, to unite. Yoga, therefore, is the science of Union. Through the practice of yoga, the soul is united with the supreme Soul. Yoga is a divine science which teaches us how to disentangle the soul from the phenomenal world of sense objects and link it with the Absolute. Yoga is a process by which individual souls can become one with the Supreme Soul.

Yoga has a recorded history of about 6,000 years in India – from the times of Mohen-jo-daro to the modern age. It has the power to satisfy the psychological and ethical needs of the modern man, whether he belongs to the East or the West, no matter if he is an atheist or an agnostic.

True yoga underlies all the major religions of the world – be it Hinduism, Christianity,

Buddhism or Islam. Through yoga one can dive deep into one's own faith and discover the great truth of the unity of all religions.

Yoga is not a theory or philosophy. Yoga is the essence of the revelation of sages and saints. Yoga is essentially a union.

But union with what?

Let us first realise that we live in a world of separateness. We are separated from our Divine Source, that which, for want of a better word, we call God. Yoga is *that* which unites man with God. Yoga is *that* which connects man with the infinite storehouse of energy that is Divinity. Yoga is *that* which transforms man and makes him God-like.

As I have surveyed the situation around me, I have found that men and women are unhappy; nations are unhappy, because they have not been able to secure a unifying vision of life. Storms may blow around me, yet I retain the inner calm of the soul, the inner rest of the heart – that is true yoga.

Yoga does not ask us to run away from the world and retire into the depths of a *tapobana* (a forest of meditation) or climb the peaks of a holy hill. Yoga is to be *in* the world, but not *of* the world. Yoga teaches us to live in the world – but not let worldliness live within us.

It was Sri Ramakrishna Paramahansa, the great yogi of India, who said: "The boat must stay on the waters. But the waters must not be allowed to enter the boat. Else the boat will sink, and we shall get drowned."

The world has been referred to by our *rishis* as the *sansar sagara*. In this ocean of the Universe, the boats of our lives must stay on the waters. But the waters of worldliness must not enter our boats. How may this be done? By entering into the depths within!

Within every one of us there are tremendous depths. When we enter into the journey inwards, we will arrive at a point where we will touch the one reality of life. The practical aspect of yoga therefore is – how to enter into the depths within. It is through meditation and concentration that we can enter into the depths that are within us.

Have you seen a convex lens? It is popularly known as the burning glass. With the help of the convex lens, the scattered rays of the sun are brought to focus at a point, and fire is produced. Ordinarily, the rays of the sun do cause fire. But because the rays are focussed, fire is produced.

Likewise our minds too, are scattered. They are dispersed through the various senses. One moment, your mind may be in London, the next moment it flies to America. If only our mind can be concentrated, one-pointed, focussed, its power would grow immensely. In addition to knowing many things in the outer world, we may know so many things of the inner realm. If our minds can be brought to one idea, one object, its power would grow immensely. Therefore, the mind is to be concentrated. Without concentration, there can be no yoga. Even if there is the slightest distraction, the God within us cannot be seen – just as the slightest break in the electric wire, puts off the electric light.

The restlessness of the mind is one of the fundamental problems which the aspirant must overcome. It is not without reason that the mind is likened to a monkey; by its nature, it is unsteady and distracted. Yoga on the other hand, requires *ekagrita* – one-pointedness of the mind. This can be achieved only through detachment and freedom from wordly desires. Rightly do experts warn us that attachment to material objects is inimical to the pursuit of yoga. There are four steps that we must take to conquer shackles of attachment:

1. Do not allow the mind to dwell on sensual pleasures or the material objects they relate to.

2. Resist desire and the temptations of desire: cultivate discrimination which can lead you to a state of *samatwa* or equanimity.

3. Overcome anger, hatred and love, which are independent of sense objects, but can still taint the mind.

4. When the senses are under control and the mind is free from likes and dislikes, the aspirant reaches the stage of independence through non-attachment. This is the stage from which spiritual progress can begin.

The *Bhagavat* gives us a memorable picture of Sukhadev, the Blessed One. Concerning Sukhadev we read that as he walked, he looked like a soldier with a fixed bayonet. His gaze did not wander; his gaze had but one goal and this goal was God. This is the meaning of yoga. If only we can understand what it is to have this gaze fixed on the goal – the great goal which is God and God alone, we have understood the meaning of *yoga*.

The *Yoga Sutras* Of Patanajali

One of the great source-books which enshrines the teachings of yoga is named *The Yoga Sutras of Patanjali*.

Who was Patanajali? He was a sage who appeared, according to some scholars, in 820 BC. The Hindu *mahakavya* (great work) of *Patanjali Charitra* gives us a truly fascinating account of the life of Patanjali. He is said to have been the incarnation of Adisesha, the sacred couch of Maha Vishnu. Adisesha expresses a desire to behold the divine spectacle of *Shiva thandava* – the ecstatic dance of Lord Shiva. To this end, he incarnates as a human being, Patanjali. Through steadfast purpose and discipline, he attains the state of *samadhi*, wherein Lord Shiva grants him the boon he desired- namely, the cosmic vision of His celestial dance. This enables Patanjali to write magnificent, authentic treatises on yoga, grammar and *ayurveda* (life science). Lord Shiva is also known as *Yogeswara* or the Lord of yoga. Thus it was the bliss of witnessing his celestial dance that enabled Patanjali to compose the masterpiece, *Yoga Sutra.*

The *Yoga Sutra* is a work in which Patanjali has brought together the *Sutras* – aphorisms – concerning the yoga of his days. He gives us the teachings in aphorisms – small, concentrated sentences – which need to be considered carefully in order to be understood.

In this book, Patanajali, a seer, a great teacher and master - speaks to us of the different stages in the development of a yogi.

The first stage, he tells us, is that of an average good man, who keeps away from the dark paths of life and lives the life of a gentleman. Yoga starts with the life of a gentleman.

Such a man refrains from all the sinful acts of life. He is good, kind, gentle, loving, helpful towards all. He harms no one, he does not indulge in any dishonest practise. He is, in short the perfect gentleman. The life of yoga, says Patanjali, begins with the life of the gentleman.

The second stage is that of the seeker, an aspirant, a *jignasu*.

The gentleman has moved along the pathways of life. He has passed through a series of experiences; he has come into contact with different types of sympathy and culture. He has served a few people, helped others. He finds that people have not understood him. They have misinterpreted his motives. Some of them have even maligned him.

He begins to ask himself: why is this happening to me? I only want to do good to people. Why do they return evil for good?

He finds too, that fortune is fickle. Money comes and goes. Nothing lasts, nothing is permanent in worldly life. The question wells up within his heart: what is the meaning of life?

Why am I here? What is the purpose of life? What is the aim of this endless adventure of existence?

He is troubled by these questions and seeks answers to them. He is anxious to know the meaning of the mystery of this unintelligible world. He wants to know the Truth about life. He becomes a *jignasu* – a seeker after Truth.

This is the second stage of yogic development.

The third stage, according to Patanjali, is a stage of the *shishya*, the disciple. The seeker sets out in search of truth. He sets out to find a sage, a seer, a saint, a yogi; a man of God, who is a teacher of wisdom, who may show him the way to the truth he seeks. He sets out in search of a *tatva darshana* - someone who has beheld and understood the secret of life; someone who has known God, who has talked and walked with Him. He sets out in quest. And, having found such a one, he sits at his feet. At the Lotus Feet of his guru he abides, drinking the wisdom that flows from the life and lips of the Master. He begins to understand the mystery that is life.

Then comes the fourth stage. The disciple has received the teaching from the Master, and he tries to live up to his teaching. Every day, in every way, he trains himself to walk on the path that the Master has pointed to him – the great guru at whose feet he has taken refuge. What are the great truths, the profound secrets he has been taught? They may not be revealed here - for they are only passed on from a true teacher to a true disciple. Suffice it to say that as a disciple puts into practise the teachings of the Master, he arrives at that blessed stage in his life, the blessed day when the grace of God is poured upon him. He beholds a light shining within him. He beholds the vision that makes him a yogi.

The fifth and final stage in the life of the yogi is God-realisation. The *shishya* becomes a *shishu* – a child of God. He beholds a glory which is difficult to describe. He is a man who has fulfilled the purpose of this human birth. He has arrived at the goal which for want of a better word we call God.

The yoga taught by Patanjali is also called the *ashtanga yoga* – the yoga of eight limbs. They are eight steps a seeker must take to tread the path of this yoga. They are *yama, niyama, asana, pranayama, pratihara, dharana, dhyana* and *samadhi*.

We should note at first, what, according to Patanjali, is yoga. He defines yoga beautifully as *chitta vriti nirodha*; *chitta* is consciousness; *vriti* is modification; *nirodha* is control. Yoga is *chitta vriti nirodha* - control of the restlessness of the mind. The mind is a stream of thoughts always going outwards. It has to be turned towards the Self, the *Atman*. The ceaseless wandering of the mind must be checked, controlled, restrained, if we would attain the only treasure that is worth having - *chitta shanti*, or peace of mind.

How may we control the mind? Eight steps must a seeker take, one after the other – the eight steps of Patanjali's *ashtanga yoga*.

1. The first is *yama*. *Yama* means, literally, control. Another word for *yama* is discipline. We must discipline our lives if we wish to advance spiritually. You cannot say, "I shall do as I like." No, there are rules you must submit to. There are disciplines you must conform to – disciplines such as *ahimsa*, non-violence, *satya*, truthfulness, *asteya*, non-stealing, *aparigraha*, non-possession, *brahmacharya*, chastity.

2. The second step is *niyama* – certain disciplines to which the seeker must conform. Time and effort must be set aside for the pursuit of these *niyamas* – cleanliness, contentment, control of the flesh, study of the scriptures.

3. The third step is *asana* – posture control and exercises that are preparatory to

meditation. These postures taught by Patanjali promote good health too. For, according to him, yoga is not for the weak, but for men and women of *shakti*.

4. The fourth step is *pranayama*, breath control. When breath is properly controlled, drawn in and let out, it helps to relax both the body and mind. *Prana* is a vital force in the air, with an enriching quality. *Pranic* energy can be conserved and utilised well by *pranayama*.

5. The fifth step is *pratihara* - restraint of the senses from sense-enjoyment. For if we wish to grow in yoga, we must resist from indulgence of the senses.

6. The sixth step is *dharana*, concentration. The mind must be undistracted and clean of everything except an all-pervading thought that helps you focus your concentration. This can be a *mantra*, an object or even an idea.

7. The seventh step is *dhyana* or meditation. We turn inwards, making our minds open and receptive to a higher consciousness. We cross the distance between ourselves and the Universal spirit. We realise a wonderful feeling of selflessness.

8. The eighth step is *samadhi* – the highest level of meditation, the supreme goal of yoga. It has been described as a state of super-consciousness. It is at-one-ment with the Universal Consciousness. *Samadhi* leads us into a world of new vision, the realisation of the One-in-all.

Abhyasis of yoga have described the *ashtanga yoga* of Patanjali as "tuning into a higher awareness". According to the system so well defined by Patanjali, yoga is a strict discipline, a learning process involving, in order, proper preparation and attitude (*yama* and *niyama*) physical and breathing exercises (*asana* and *pranayama*), control of the senses (*pratihara*), concentration (*dharana*), contemplation (*dhyana*) and meditation (*samadhi*).

Types Of Yoga

There are different types of yoga. There is *gyana yoga*, *dhyana yoga*, *prapatti yoga*, *samatva yoga*, *surat-shabda yoga* – but all these and more are brought together under four main categories.

The first main category of yoga is that which we call *mantra yoga*. *Mantra* yoga teaches us how concentration can be achieved by the repetition of a single word or a set of words or even a single syllable, which is symbolic of God or Truth.

The power of the Word is celebrated by all the religions of the world. Sant Tulsidas tells us: "Even when repeated in a careless manner, the Name Divine burns up all accumulated negative *Karma*. But when it is repeated with feeling and devotion, it can help the devotee cross the ocean of the world-process." That is why great importance is given to *mantra japa* in yoga. Repetition of a *mantra* is one of the most effective techniques of spiritual discipline.

A *mantra* works on several levels. At the literal level, a *mantra* is a brief prayer – e.g. *Om Namo Shivaya*, or *Om Namo Bhagavate Vasudevaya*. But at a deeper level, every *mantra* is also a mystic formulation, which has come down to us from our *rishis* and seers. The very letters (*akshara*) and sounds (*shabda*) of which the *mantra* is composed, are packed with a mystic, spiritual energy, which influences the mind, heart and soul of those who repeat it.

You may take up any name, any syllable, any line, which is dear to you, and which is symbolic of God and symbolic of Truth. There is that ancient Vedic syllable, which is so dear to many of us in India – the ancient basic *mantra*, A…U…M…Take it up, repeat it again and again with deep emotion, deep feeling of the heart. It will lead you eventually, to the point at which, losing yourself, you will find the

Beloved; you will find the Lord seated in the Lotus of the heart.

Take up any name that draws you, any syllable. God is the Nameless One, but the sages have called Him by many Names. All these forms, all these names point to the One Lord. We need not quarrel over the Names. We can call upon Him by any Name we choose. Call Him Rama – the Name that is dear to the Soul of India. Call Him Shyama – the Name that was dear to the hearts of the Gopis of Vrija. Call Him Jesus, call Him Allah, call Him Yehovah, call Him Ahura Mazda.

There is the *Maha Mantra:*

> *Hare Rama, Hare Rama, Rama, Rama, Hare, Hare,*
>
> *Hare Krishna, Hare Krishna, Krishna, Krishna, Hare, Hare!*

You can invoke Him by any *mantra*. The Buddhists invoke the great cosmic power by the *mantra, Om mani padmehum.* Every religion invokes the Great Power in its own way. Repeat your chosen *mantra* with love and deep devotion – and you will find peace descending within you.

Japa yoga – the technique of repetition of the *mantra* – can be practised at any time. Many people do it before they fall asleep at night, or as they wake up every morning. There are people who keep repeating the chosen *mantra* throughout the day, whenever they are not absorbed by work. Such a practice soon becomes second nature with them, and they find themselves drawn to the *mantra* subconsciously, whenever their mind seeks rest and peace.

Likhit Japa – writing your chosen *mantra* over and over again – is an effective *sadhana* which brings about purity of mind and concentration. Even one page a day will help develop patience, steadiness and relaxation.

Repeating or writing the *mantra* is a technique of yoga that is open to us all. It evokes positive, spiritual vibrations in us; it brings us grace; it purifies the mind and strengthens the body. It helps us to build up a reserve of mental, emotional and spiritual power that will take us to the path of self–realisation.

The second main category of yoga is *raja yoga*. This aims at the control of the breath and the mind. As the name indicates, *raja yoga* is the royal yoga. It is the yoga of meditation. It is said to have been developed by the Aryan civilisation.

According to the ancient philosophy of *raja yoga,* each one of us is blessed with infinite potential, laying open for us endless possibilities. So it is that Lord Krishna tells his dear disciple, Arjuna in the Bhagavad Gita:

> *The yogi is greater than the ascetic; the yogi is even greater that the Vedic scholar; the yogi is greater than the man of rituals. Therefore, do*

thou become a yogi, O Arjuna!

And of all yogis, he who, full of faith adoreth Me, with his self abiding in Me – he is deemed by Me to be the most completely harmonised!

Even such is the *raja yogi* – one who has mastered the technique of *raja yoga*.

The next category of yoga, is *hatha yoga* or the yoga of physical culture. It is, in a sense, a branch of *raja yoga*. It is said to be a total and a complete system of psycho-physical training, which helps to harmonise mind and body with the external world and the elements with which all creation is composed. It is thought that the system of *hatha-yoga* was developed by the ancient civilisation of Lemuria – a continent which has now disappeared from the face of the earth.

Hatha yoga is based on a system of exercises which include the following:

• *Asanas* or various postures

- *Pranayama* or breathing exercises

- *Mudras* or special poses

- *Bandhas* or "ties" involving concentration

- *Kriyas* or purificatory exercises

Exponents of *hatha yoga* claim that through exercises, concentration and meditation, the *kundalini shakti* (the coiled-up energy that lies dominant within us) can be unfolded, and ultimately, a union with the Divine achieved.

However that may be, we see today that some people who practise *hatha yoga* are interested more in physical power rather than spiritual progress. So it is that they spend all their energy in displaying marvellous feats - such as remaining buried under the earth for days together; stopping their heartbeats at will; drinking acid or swallowing pieces of glass. However impressive such displays may be to the common man, it must be emphasised that they are unholy practices – and they can have no relationships with true spiritual life.

Laya yoga teaches us to attain peace and serenity at the very core of the inner consciousness. The word "laya" signifies void or emptiness – the absolute dissolution of the ego. The symbol of *laya yoga* is the lotus of one thousand petals, with a void in the centre. It is a system of meditation which all of us can practise. It is a process of spiritual ascent and descent, made by concentrating on the lotus in each *chakra* of the body and observing them with detachment. The various stages of *laya yoga* are as follows:

1. The practitioner begins with the lotus, *Muladhara* - at the base of the spine. As he concentrates on this lotus he finds its petals opening. He perceives his body as separate from the Self, and he begins to experience freedom.

2. Thus detached, he observes the lotus, *swadisthana* – the centre of the ego and the

vital forces. He becomes aware of the instincts, and the role they play in life. Observing them with detachment, he experiences emancipation from them.

3. Next he observes the lotus *manipura* – representing the five senses. The senses have brought to him the varied experiences of the world. At times, they have overwhelmed his life by their uncontrolled power. Now, detached observation gives him freedom from the senses.

4. As a dispassionate observer, he looks at the lotus, *anahata* – the symbol of the mind. Its petals open to disclose the feelings of pride, possession, demands, desires and expectations that throng his mind. He isolates himself from these feelings and feels he is a free observer.

5. In this free sensation, he observes the lotus, *vishuddha*, the seat of pure intellect. He watches how the intellect has dominated

his life with its ideas. A wide vista of universal existence now opens up before him, and the narrow ideas of the intellect are discarded.

6. Now he observes the lotus *ajna* – at the centre of the eyebrows. He regards his own ego, around which his entire life has been built. It is linked with all that he has left behind – the intellect, mind, senses, instincts and the body. He rises above the ego – and glimpses endless, limitless calm.

7. Finally, he arrives at the lotus *sahasra* – the thousand petalled lotus at whose core lies the void he wishes to reach. Its petals represent the whole universe. He reaches the peak of his ascent and feels a sense of completion and fulfilment by knowing the true nature of his self, his freedom and universality. He experiences tranquility, freedom and oneness with all life.

The contemplation, having passed through the steps of Ascent, now follows the steps of Descent. The practitioner is left with a sense of well-being, assurance and fulfillment.

Any *yoga* aspirant can create his own form of meditation with *laya yoga*.

It is said that the inhabitants of Atlantis, a legendary continent in which an ideal civilisation flourished long, long ago, evolved this system of *laya* yoga to develop their psychic power.

Kundalini yoga: In Sanskrit, *Kundalini* literally means "snake" or "snake power". This refers to the latent superior force in every human being, which is thought to lie curled at the base of the spine. This force is awakened from sleep through *kundalini* yoga, and it rises through a series of centers or *chakras* to attain spiritual awareness.

This is a highly technical process which can be learnt only at the feet of a competent guide.

The Yoga Of The Gita

The *yoga* that is dear to the heart of the *Krishna Bhakta* – the devotee of Lord Sri Krishna – is the *ashtanga yoga,* which the Bhagavad Gita spells out for us. For the Gita is not only a text of spiritual culture, but is also a great book of yogic culture. And *ashtanga yoga* – a yoga of eight limbs – is outlined by the Lord in the Gita: the eight limbs being *karma, gyana, dhyana, bhakti, asanga, samatwa, samadhrishti* – and the ultimate final step *sharanam.*

1. Karma, the first step, is that of desireless action. The aspirant at this stage is one who acts, but acts with detachment. He works, but has no desire for rewards. He lives in the world, but is unstained by worldly life. Without renouncing action, he offers all his work as devotion to the Lord.

The *Karma marga* trains the aspirant to regard his body, mind and the sense-organs not as his, but as instruments of the Lord. This purifies his *antahkarana* or inner instrument, and he learns to serve selflessly, abandoning all attachment.

2. *Gyana*, the second step, is the step of true wisdom. This wisdom is the knowledge of the *atman*, the true Self within. Even as the sun dispels all darkness, the light of wisdom disperses all ignorance and reveals the Supreme to the true yogi.

The aspirant learns to live and move in the Supreme. He meditates on *That* and is devoted to *That*. When he leaves the mortal body he reaches the abode from which there is no return to the wheel of birth and death.

The true *gnani*, or *tatva gnani*, is called the *mahatma* or the great soul. Such a great soul, says Lord Krishna, is rare to find. He is a product of a long evolutionary process. Having practised *yagna*, *tapas*, *daan* and *satsang* through a series of births, he has purified his *antahkarana*, and become a *mahatma*. Such a great soul is one, in understanding and will, with the Lord.

3. *Dhyana*, the third step, is that of meditation. It helps you develop a new focus of attention. By concentrating on your *Ishtadevata*, you will gradually become attuned to the Divine Will. *Dhyana* or meditation is commitment to the self, the *Atman*, to Truth.

Discipline is essential for *dhyana marga*. When you meditate on the Lord or concentrate on one of his teachings, it will become an avenue to the Divine Spirit. This discipline may be sought from a guru, or from an inspired scripture. Group meditation may also be practised in the *satsang*.

In meditation you must seek to be receptive. Relaxation must lead you from effort to effortlessness; from concious activity to silence; from the superfices of life to the depths within.

When this point is reached, the inner being of the spirit is revealed: and every moment of your inner life becomes a part of eternity.

4. *Bhakti*, the fourth step, is that of devotion. Sadhu Vaswani described *bhakti* as the will-to-love.

The will-to-live is the dominant note of western civilisation: and this civilisation is afflicted with greed, conflict, violence and war. For the will-to-live is a desire for power.

The *bhakta* is one who rises above desire, to the desireless state of love. This gives him the aspiration to forget himself and embrace the inner life of the *atman*.

The *bhakta* is one who aspires to surrender all he is and has to the One Life, to take refuge at the Lotus Feet of the Lord.

The Lord identifies four types of *bhaktas* who come to him for various reasons:

- The *artha bhaktas* are the afflicted ones. They seek the Lord's protection in their distress.

- The *artharthi bhaktas* are those who seek success in their undertakings. They may want power or possession; they may seek the heaven-world after death. They look up to God to grant them success in their endeavour.

- The *jignasu bhaktas* are those who do not seek money or pleasure, but seek Light and Truth. They pray to the Lord for illumination.

- The *gnani bhakta* or the wise devotee, seeks nothing less than God-realisation. For him God is the goal Supreme.

The other three *bhaktas* are swayed by desire; but the *gnani bhakta* in his wisdom, is emancipated from desire and seeks the essence of the universe – God.

5. *Asangha,* the fifth step, is that of detachment. One of the greatest concepts in the Gita is detachment: desirelessness. The aspirant at this stage, eliminates affection and attachment for that which is created. He empties his heart of all created things; he eliminates habits, impulses, affections and attachments which hinder the way to perfect life: much talking, affection for an individual, fondness for books or food or even literary or artistic pursuits. He makes an offering of his life to God, and grows in the grace of God.

6. *Samatwa,* the sixth step, is that of equanimity. *Samatwa* is not attainable by those whose minds are restless. But even the restless mind can be curbed and conquered by *abhyasa* (practice) and *vairagya* (dispassion). These can lead to self-control, which is vital for the attainment of this rare and difficult state. It is attained by one who ceaselessly strives to bring the mind under control. This is done by the following *sadhanas:*

- Renounce desire

- Cultivate *ekagrita* – one-pointedness of the mind

- Endeavour to see the One-in-all

- Be aware that one is not the body that one wears

- Be conscious of the transience of all life

- Concentrate on the *ishtadevta* and *japa* of the chosen Name

- Bear witness to your worship in purified actions – selfless service in your daily life

7. *Samadhrishti*, the seventh step, is equalmindedness – in joy and sorrow, sun and rain, in loss and gain, in pleasure and pain. It is the mark of him who is a *yoga yukta* – he who realises that the One *atman* is in all, and that the beauty of God that awakes in the hearts of his *bhaktas* is beyond *tapas*, *daan* and the *scriptures*.

To the man of *samadhrishti,* the seer and the seen are but one. To him every bud and blossom, every berry and every blade of grass, every laurel and every lily, every stream and every sea, every vineyard and every valley – is a manifestation of the One Divine Self.

The *Samadarshi* is free from preference, prejudice and predilection. He sees the One Self in the cow, the elephant or the dog; he beholds Krishna in the selfless *brahmin* and the humble outcast. He rests in the Eternal, who is the *Samam* (balanced).

8. *Sharanam,* the ultimate, final step, represents the quintessence of the dedicated life. The Gita teaches us how to live a life of dedication, *arpanam* to the Eternal. The best gift one can give is not money; the best gift one can give is the gift of oneself. Surrender yourself, completely, unconditionally, joyfully to the Eternal – and you will achieve salvation. Out of the energy released through *arpanam,* arise great things – within and without.

Give yourself to the Lord, and he will make you an impersonal instrument of mighty forces for the highest good of humanity. You will then belong not to yourself but to the World-Purpose. True happiness lies in emancipation through *arpanam* – self-surrender – to the Lord. And so it is that the Lord promises us in the Bhagavad Gita:

> *Renouncing all rites and writ duties, come unto Me alone for single refuge. Do not grieve for I shall liberate you from all bondage to sin and suffering. Of this have no doubt.*

(XVII,66)

Sri Krishna also tells us in the Gita:

> *The yogi is greater than the ascetic; the yogi is greater than the Vedic scholar; the yogi is greater than the man of rituals.* (VI,46)

The ascetic (*tapasvi*) inflicts severe penances on his body; but greater than the *tapasvi* is the yogi.

The *gnani* (knower of the Vedas) is great; but greater than the *gnani* is the yogi.

The *karmi* (man of action) too, is great; but greater than him is a true yogi.

Tapasya, gnana, karma are all aids to spiritual unfolding; but all three find their fulfillment in the true yogi – the *ashtanga yogi* – who lives perpetually in the divine presence. He beholds Krishna in himself, and sees Krishna in all.

And the best of yogis, according to the Gita, is he who offers to the Lord his love, who gives his heart to the Lord and worships Him in faith and love.

Practical Suggestions

I would wish to pass on to you a few practical suggestions which I have found useful in the pursuit of yoga. I love to call it the *sahaj yoga* – the simple yoga. For yoga is nothing unnatural. Yoga is not foreign to us. Yoga is like the return of an intoxicated man to a life of sobriety. Having come to this world of allurements and entanglements, so many of us have drunk the wine of *maya*. A veil of ignorance – *avidya* – clouds our minds. It is this ignorance that robs the intellect of its knowledge of discrimination. One begins to think that he is the body, the mind, the senses. One confounds the perishable body to be the spirit and starts hankering after pleasure. In reality this world of *maya* is nothing but a source of misery. When we are satisfied by worldly pleasures, its possessions and its powers, we begin to live an existence similar to that of animals. From *maya* – intoxication, man has to attain God-intoxication. Ignorance has to be destroyed by the knowledge of the Self.

This is where yoga helps. The true yogi sees the world as a manifestation of God and though he discharges his day-to-day duties, he is not attached to any object or condition. He becomes a master of his circumstances.

Napoleon's soldiers were marching across the African desert. They were famished by the heat, and overcome by thirst. As they trudged forward, someone from the fore ranks shouted, "Water! Here is water!"

Eagerly, the soldiers scanned the vast desert ahead. Far ahead of them, towards the horizon, they saw what appeared to be a lake. Its waters shimmered and sparkled in the brilliant sunshine.

Mad with relief, the soldiers rushed forward in the direction of the "waters". But as they raced towards it, it receded. To their utter dismay, that which seemed to be a lake of refreshing waters was nothing but a mirage in the desert!

The illusory, passing, deceiving pleasures of this world too, are only a mirage – a vision of *maya*.

To come out of the veil of *avidya* the following suggestions may prove helpful:

Practical suggestion No. 1

Yoga is not taught. It is caught. *Asanas* can be taught, *pranayama* can be taught, but yoga is not taught. It is caught through fellowship with a Master yogi – a yogi who lives in constant communion with the Eternal. If you can find one such yogi – go and sit at his feet, gaze at his radiant face, look into the depths of his eyes, and catch the vibrations that flow out of him in an endless stream. Receive those vibrations, bathe in those vibrations.

The vibrations that emanate from a true yogi will inspire and uplift you. Even though a yogi may not be doing tangible or visible things, he is igniting the spark in you and nurturing it just by his vibrations. Although he may not be speaking aloud or performing actions, he creates an atmosphere which will help you to progress on the path.

In the great epic *Ramayana,* we are told how the *vanaras* (monkeys) fought the demons everyday. At the end of the day, they were injured, afflicted, miserable and depressed. At the time of evening twilight, they gathered in the presence of Sri Rama who simply looked at them. With his powerful vibrations, healing emanated from his gaze and healed and re-strenghtened the monkeys who were now ready to fight the demons the next day.

Sri Rama did not say a word, he did not lay his hands on the monkeys; just his mere gaze alleviated their sufferings and they felt refreshed and renewed.

Therefore always aspire to come into contact with a Master yogi. Do not go out in quest of him. He will come to you at the right time.

Continue to long for him. Just as a ship needs a captain, so too, the boats of our lives need the guidance of true yogi to reach the other shore – else the boat will be carried by the angry waves of lust, desire, greed. The boat will be battered and torn. When you have his guidance, gradually you will find that the level of your consciousness will keep rising higher, until one blessed day, under the grace of the yogi you will be blessed with a vision of God in the lotus of your heart.

Practical suggestion No. 2

Practise silence everyday. Everyday spare some little time and delve deep within yourself. For it is only in and through silence that we can cleanse ourselves. Silence is a great purifier. It is only when our minds are purified that we can behold the beauteous face of God.

An anxious disciple went to a spiritual master and said, "A deep desire has arisen within me for God-realisation. Pray, show me the way to *mukti* – liberation. Grant me the gift of emancipation."

The guru quietly replied, "In order to fulfil your wish, you will have to come and stay for a period of time with me, follow my instructions and surely you will attain enlightenment."

"This is the jet age," the disciple interrupted, "a computer age. Why can't you give me enlightenment right now?"

The guru thought for a moment and said to him, "I am glad you are eager to receive enlightenment. Let us first try to get a little familiar with each other. If you will permit me, tonight I will come and have dinner with you."

The aspirant jumped at the idea. At night the guru arrived at the residence of the aspirant. Immediately he said to the aspirant, "I am eager to eat. Kindly put all the dishes you have cooked into my begging bowl."

The aspirant looked into the begging bowl and saw that it already had some stale, left over articles of food.

"Let me wash the bowl first," he said.

"I am too hungry. I cannot wait. Forget about washing the bowl, be quick and serve me with the food," the guru insisted.

"But I have made everything with so much effort - great care has been taken to cook a delicious meal for you. The good food will get polluted if it is put in this filthy, unwashed bowl!"

Quietly answered the guru: "If this food can't be served until the vessel is clean – how can I put enlightenment - the food of knowledge - into your mind which is not pure? First purify the mind through practice of silence!"

A pure mind is like a dry matchstick. It ignites the moment you strike it. But if the matchstick is wet, however hard you may strike it, it will not light. Similarly the mind soiled by worldliness can be purified by silence.

Preferably at the same time and at the same place practise silence, for when the time and place are the same, it builds for you a focus and into this focus come forces from above which help to still the mind.

Sit in silence and recall an incident from the life of a great one of humanity – Krishna, Rama, Jesus, Moses, Buddha, Baha u' llah, Guru Nanak. All are but forms of the One Eternal Spirit.

Or take up a symbol – the Flute of Sri Krishna, the Cross of Jesus, the Lotus of the Buddha and concentrate on the symbol.

Or take up a Name of God which is dear to you. All names belong to Him who is the Nameless One.

It makes no difference by what name or form you worship Him. Sri Ramakrishna used to say, "Sweetened bread will taste sweet in whatever way you eat it." Plunge into silence, dive deep and you are sure to find the eternal treasure.

As you tread the path of silence there comes a stage where you forget the name, the form and the symbol as you enter into the Formless. And you are filled with the joy that no ending knows, the peace that passeth, surpasseth, understanding.

Practical Suggestion No. 3

Shun all desire for personal popularity. Let your mind and heart be filled with the love of God so that there is no place in it for egoism, vanity, popularity. Remember God is very close to man, but man is far removed from God. It is the veil of the ego that separates man from God. As soon as the veil of the ego is pierced, man beholds God, face-to-face.

A young man was much given to pride and arrogance. He received a medal in the college.

The man who bestowed the medal on him used extravagant language to praise him and his accomplishments.

The young man's head and heart were swollen with pride.

That night, when he went home, he repeated the words of praise he received, to his mother. Having delivered a glowing tribute to himself, he asked her, "How many great men are there in the world today, anyhow?"

The mother, a wise old woman, looked at him with pity and said, "One less than you think!"

Truly, ego can blind us to the truth about ourselves.

A proud lawyer told a farmer, "I never bow my head before anyone – neither God nor man!"

The wise farmer replied, "Can you see that field of grain? Only the heads of grain that are empty, stand upright. The well-filled ones bow low!"

A proud lady arrived late at a concert and found that she could be seated only in one of the back rows, for the hall was full.

Angry and insulted, she said to the organisers, "You obviously do not know how to seat your guests properly!"

"Not at all, madam," said one of them, "Those who matter don't mind where they sit. Those who mind, don't matter to us!"

Dissociate yourself from the ego. Until you have liberated yourself from this false identification you will be bound.

The sage Patanjali gives a beautiful illustration of an absolutely pure crystal. It doesn't have any colour of its own. However, if you put a chrysanthemum close to the crystal, the crystal will look yellowish. Bring a pink flower close to it and the crystal will look pinkish. Don't forget that the crystal is *not* pink – it appears to be pink because of its association with the pink flower. The moment you separate the flower and the crystal, the crystal will look clear and pure.

Similarly our mind is crystal clear and pure. But it attaches, identifies itself with the body and the senses. It is only when you dissociate yourself from them, that you attain liberation.

Take out a parrot from an iron cage and put it in a golden cage – do you think it will be happy? It will say: a cage is a cage – whether it is of iron or gold.

Unless and until you totally free yourself from the ego you will be bound.

When ego is given prominence in one's life, the mind is crippled. However, when the mind rises above the ego – it begins to focus more and more on God.

Someone asked Socrates, "Why is it that Alcibiades is so unhappy? He has travelled much, seen much of the world, and is so gifted too!"

The sage answered, "True it is, that he has travelled a lot. Wherever he goes he takes himself with him. That is the cause of his misery."

Practical Suggestion No. 4

The seeker of yoga is not a social reformer. He is not out to reform others – for he knows that the best way to reform the world is to reform oneself. It was Carlyle who said: "O Bobus, reform Thyself." If you want to reform the world – begin with yourself. Such a one knows that a living example is worth more than a thousand discourses. He becomes a self-reformer.

It was Swami Ramtirth who inserted an advertisement in *The Tribune* of Lahore which read:

WANTED REFORMERS

Underneath were the words in very thin type:

Who are prepared to reform themselves.

He did not get an answer to his advertisement.

It is said, "Holiness vanishes when you talk about it, becomes conspicuous when you live it."

Let us not talk of yoga, let us live yoga. Let us become living, moving pictures of yoga.

Bayazid, the great Sufi, says about himself: "I was a revolutionary when I was young and my prayer to God was: Lord give me the energy to change the world.

"As I approached middle age, I realised that half my life was gone without my changing a single soul on earth. I therefore, altered my prayer to God: Lord, give me the strength to change all those who come in contact with me – just my family and close friends.

"Now that I am old and my life is drawing to a close, my prayer to God is, Lord, give me the grace to change myself.

"If I would have prayed for this right since my youth, I would have not wasted my life."

Let us reform, re-form ourselves!

Practical Suggestion No. 5

Whatever you do, make of it an offering to the Lord. Whatever you do, do it only to please God.

The Master says in the Bhagavad Gita: "Whatever you eat, whatever you give in charity, whatever austerity you practise, whatever you do, O Arjuna, make it an offering unto Me." Even a simple act such as eating can be offered to the Lord. When we offer what we eat to the Lord – the mark is that if some day we get food which is not to our taste, we do not complain.

Whatever you do, offer it to God. Say to Him: I am not the doer. I am but a broken instrument. If there are mistakes done, they are mine. But all glory belongs to Thee.

Therefore stop saying I did it. This is mine. I earned it. Instead say: Everything is Thine. The energy is Thine. Nothing belongs to me. I am Thine.

There are a hundred and one ways of doing the same thing. Are you a professor teaching in classroom? Are you a lawyer arguing a case in a court of law? Are you a doctor attending to patients? There are many ways of doing the same thing. Some are right, some are wrong. But only one is the best! And because you are doing everything for the love of God, because you are doing everything as an offering unto the Lord, you must do your work in the best way possible.

It was an Arabian poet who said: "Are you a mason building a house? Build it in the aspiration that some day perhaps the Beloved will come and dwell in your home. How much love would you not put into the building of such a house!

"Are you a weaver working at the loom, weaving a piece of cloth? Weave the cloth in the hope that the cloth will be worn by the Beloved. How much love would you not pour into your weaving!"

There was a painter who painted pictures of fascinating beauty. One day as he was painting, a friend happened to drop in. The artist was painting a beautiful portrait of Sri Krishna. The friend stood spell–bound. The painting captivated his heart.

"Do you like the picture?" enquired the artist.

"Yes, I not only like but I admire the picture. You could not have painted such a beautiful face of the Lord until you loved Him!" said the friend, with deep admiration.

"Love Him!" echoed the artist, "Of course I do. And the more I love him, the better will I paint Him and the more fascinating will the picture become!"

Yes, if we do anything for the love of God – it turns out to be the best. Therefore, every action should be done in a spirit of offering to the Lord!

Practical Suggestion No. 6

See that you do nothing which may rob you of your peace of mind. Inner rest of the soul, is your richest treasure. Regulate your life in such a way that it adds to your inner calm and does not take away your peace. Therefore, avoid overwork. And do not be in a hurry to do anything.

Attend to your duties gently, lovingly, trustingly. Never feel upset. Do not be angry with anyone. Remember peace is your richest treasure – let nothing, no one take it from you.

When Plato, the great thinker, was told that the boys in the street were making fun of his singing, he said: "Aye, then I must learn to sing better!"

There was a great man who did not allow criticism to disturb his calm! In fact he used it as a stepping-stone.

On another occasion Plato was told, "Are you aware, Sir, you have many critics?" Calmly Plato replied: "It does not matter, I will so live that none shall believe them."

Practical Suggestion No. 7

Take care of your *sangha*. Seek the company of good people and the holy ones. The more you move in the association of such people, the more you will find that love and longing wakes up in your heart. Shun worldly company – for it drags you down to worldly concerns.

When you move in the company of *bhaktas* – the lovers of the Lord – you will catch the spark of Love from them and your heart will be afire with purity and aspiration.

Satsang helps you to overcome your negative emotions. It fills you with positive vibrations and the energy you require to overcome ignorance, temptations and evil.

Life on earth is like a journey through a dark and dense forest. The company of good people is like a lamp that will light your way across this forest so that you may reach your destination safely.

An ancient legend tells us a memorable story about the power of *satsang*. Once, Rishi Narada approached Lord Vishnu and requested him humbly: "My Lord! Do tell me about the value and influence of *satsang*. I am eager to know what it can do for the seeker."

Lord Vishnu smiled at Narada. He said, "I am so busy now, I do not have the time to talk to you about it. But I would like to help you. Please go to the giant banyan tree in the forest located at the foot of the Meru Hills. There you will find a squirrel. He will enlighten you about *satsang*."

Rishi Narada was puzzled. A squirrel – to enlighten him on *satsang*! But the Lord's word was absolute, and Narada did as he was told. He found the tree in question, and a lively squirrel jumped down before him.

In all respect, Narada said to him, "I pray you, dear squirrel, enlighten me on the value and influence of *satsang*." The squirrel looked at Narada with its beady, bright eyes for what seemed to be a long drawn out minute. Narada looked into its eyes and held his gaze. At the end of the minute the squirrel curled up, lifeless. It was dead!

Taken aback, Narada found his way back to *Vaikunth*, where he narrated the moving incident to the Lord. "I hope I have not been instrumental in the death of the poor creature," he lamented. "And, dear Lord, my question is still unanswered. Wilt Thou enlighten me?"

"I'm afraid that's not possible Narada," replied the Lord. "Go back to the same tree. You will find a monkey, who will give you the knowledge you seek."

Faithfully, Narada did as he was told. Indeed, he found the monkey swinging from one branch to another. When he saw Narada, the monkey jumped down with a thud.

"I pray you, O monkey, to enlighten me on the value of *satsang*," Narada said to the monkey respectfully.

The monkey drew close and looked deep into Narada's eyes. In a minute, he dropped dead at the sage's feet.

This time, Narada was nonplussed. In utter shock, he rushed to Lord Vishnu and said: "Lord, I do not know what is wrong. The monkey you mentioned has also dropped dead before my eyes. What am I doing to these poor creatures? Who will now enlighten me on the *satsang*?"

"Well, Narada," said Lord Vishnu. "Tomorrow a prince will be born in the royal family of the kingdom in which the forest is located. Go and bless the new born child – and he will enlighten you on the matter you seek."

"But...my Lord..." stammered Narada. "When I consider the fate of the squirrel... and the monkey... how can I dare to approach this innocent, newborn baby?"

"Do you or don't you need enlightenment on *satsang*?" asked the Lord with a smile. "Go to the child. Your quest will be fulfilled."

It was with a trembling heart that Narada entered the royal palace the next morning. The King and Queen were deeply honoured to see him. They welcomed him with all ceremony that was due to a *maharishi*. They entreated him to bless their newborn son – the heir to the throne.

Rishi Narada was taken to the room where the baby prince lay asleep in the cradle. His heart beat fast as he laid his hand on the brow of the child to bless him.

No sooner had he touched the child, than the baby opened its eyes and looked deep into the eyes of the Rishi.

"O Prince," said Rishi Narada, a cold sweat breaking out over his forehead. "Lord Vishnu bade me come to you to ask you about the value of the *satsang*."

To the rishi's utter amazement, the baby began to speak. "Rishi Narada, you see me here – the manifest proof of the value of *satsang*. In my previous births, I was a squirrel, and then a monkey. As a squirrel, I was only motivated by appetite. I did nothing but gather and hoard. When I met you and looked into your eyes, I was released from that birth. My *karma* caused me to take birth as a monkey. Then again, I had the good fortune to encounter you at close quarters. Released from that incarnation, I have risen in the scale of evolution to take birth as a Prince in the pious family of the King of this country. If one minute in the company of a holy one like you could help me this far, I leave you to judge what the value and influence of sustained *satsang* can be!"

Rishi Narada was overjoyed. The Lord had indeed performed a *leela* to teach his humble devotee the value of *satsang*.

Practical Suggestion No. 8

Many of us are anxious to measure our progress on the path of yoga. There is no scale for self-measurement. Let your life grow deeper and deeper. Let your meditation grow from more to more. Therefore, speak little, eat little and sleep little. At night keep awake and meditate. And during the day give the service of Love to all. The day on which you have not brought comfort to a comfortless one, joy into the life of a joyless one, is a lost day indeed!

Myths About Yoga

Many people believe that yoga is for old people. On the contrary yoga is for all – men and women, young and old.

It is young people who should take to the practice of yoga for it will ensure good health and flexibility in old age. When you take to yoga at a young age, you will acquire suppleness and vitality which will strengthen the body.

It is often thought that practitioners of yoga are ascetics and men of renunciation who live a life of contemplation and solitude. But this is not true. Businessmen, students, athletes, executives and housewives have found that *yoga* changes their life for the better.

Of late, *hatha yoga* or a programme of physical postures has become very popular with people in the west and the east. This has led to the misconception that yoga has only to do with the body. We must not forget that physical well-being or fitness is only a step towards spiritual well-being. It must be emphasised that the ultimate goal of yoga is union with God.

Yoga is used by a few people to perform *siddhis* – display various powers that normal individuals cannot attain. The exponents who perform these *siddhis* are often taken to be men of tremendous spiritual attainment.

This is not strictly true. Patanjali tells us that these *siddhis* can be acquired by all who practise yoga regularly and faithfully. These are just milestones along the highway of yoga. We should not mistake them for the destination.

Due to the rising popularity of yoga, it has now become fashionable for people to undertake one-week, two-week or even crash courses in yoga. Unfortunately, many of them drop the exercises shortly after the course. Such half-hearted attempts will never bring you the true benefits of yoga.

There is an old proverb that says, "If wealth is lost, nothing is lost. If health is lost everything is lost."

The foundation of a healthy body is a healthy mind. It is only when body and mind function in harmony that man can lead a happy, healthy life.

The ancient sages tell us: *Shariram Brahma Mandiram* – The body is a temple of the Lord. If this be so, then it is essential we maintain this temple of the body as best as we can – in purity, cleanliness and good shape.

Hatha Yoga

Hatha yoga, as we have said is a complete system of psycho-physical training. It includes *asanas*, *kriyas*, *mudras* and *bandhas*. You should never stretch your body beyond its natural limits to perform any of these exercises. You must practise them steadily, gradually and build them up stage-by-stage. When you have completed a series of *asanas*, you should feel refreshed, renewed, energised. This is the indication that you have carried out the yogic exercises well. If on the other hand you feel tired, drained out and low, you have stretched yourself beyond the natural limits of your body, and the exercises are not likely to do you any good.

Here are a few helpful hints which you can follow when you begin a programme of yogic exercises:

1. As far as possible, you should perform your exercises on an empty stomach. The early hours of the morning are best suited for this purpose. If you are unable to do your exercises in the morning ensure that there is at least a three-hour gap after a meal.

2. To begin with, do not practise yogic exercises on a hard floor. You may, if you like, use a carpet or a folded towel.

3. Wear loose-fitting, comfortable clothes that will not impede your movements.

4. The room you use should be well-lit and well-ventilated. Many regular practitioners prefer to do their early morning exercise outdoors.

5. Chant the "Om" *mantra* or any other *mantra* before you begin your yogic exercise programme. It will help to calm your nerves, soothe the mind and help to build your power of concentration.

6. Relax between each *asana* or exercise and practise deep breathing.

7. Follow the subtle message of your body, to determine the duration of each posture or exercise. Do not strain or over-exert yourself, just to keep up a particular posture for a long time.

8. Be as regular as possible with your exercise routine. This is the key to success in *yoga*.

A few simple exercises:

Here are a few guidelines, step-by-step directions, laid out by yoga experts for beginners who wish to practise a few basic *asanas*:

1. *Surya Namaskar,* as the name implies is worship of the Sun. It helps to increase the flexibility of the body, and to make our breathing rhythmic.

   • Face the sun, palms together in front of the chest. Stand erect with feet together. Relax and breath out.

SURYA NAMASKAR

(12 Poses)

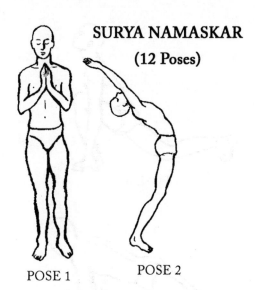

POSE 1

POSE 2

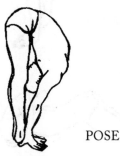

POSE 3

POSE 4

POSE 5

POSE 6

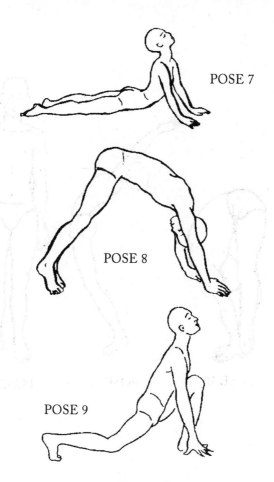

POSE 7

POSE 8

POSE 9

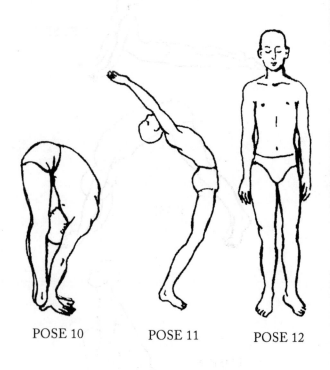

POSE 10   POSE 11   POSE 12

- Breathe in and raise the arms over the head. Bend backwards as far as possible.

- Breathe out and bend forward. Place the hands on the feet or on the ground, and bring the forehead towards the knees.

- Breathe in and move the right leg away from the body in a big, backward step, with the knee on the ground. Keep the palms and left foot in line in front and firmly on the ground. Bend the head backwards and lower the hips.

- Hold the breath. Move the left leg backwards also keeping the feet together and knees off the ground.

- Rest only on the hands and feet, the arms must be straight and the body and the legs in a straight line.

- Breathe out and lower only the knees, chest and forehead to the ground. Keep the buttocks raised up.

- Breathe in and raise the head and trunk off the ground. Bend the spine back. Keep the legs and pelvis on the ground.

- Breathe out and, without moving the feet and hands raise the body, strengthen the back and the legs and place the heels on the ground. The back and legs form an inverted "V".

- Breathe in and bring the right foot forward. Place it in line with the hands. Keep the left knee on the ground. Look up and bend the back.

- Breathe out and bring the left leg forward. Straighten the legs, especially the knees. Bring the forehead to the knees.

- Breathe in and, raising the arms over the head, bend back.

- Breathe out and return to normal position, arms at the side. Stand erect and relax.

2. *Sarvaang asana* – is a posture that helps us to exercise all the parts of our body. It is regarded as a wholesome body–building exercise.

Technique:

- Lie on the back with the hands along the sides.   Slowly breathe in and raise the legs upwards. Support the hips with the hands. Gradually raise the trunk, hips and legs to a vertical position until you rest only on the shoulders and neck.   Rest   the

sarvangasana

elbows firmly on the ground and support the back with both hands.

- Press the chin against the chest. Breathe slowly. Focus the attention on the thyroid, just below the chin. Keep this position steadily as long as comfortable. On coming out of the *asana*, slowly lower the legs to the ground without any jerks.

3. *Bhujang asana* – is a posture that resembles the position of a cobra with a raised head. It helps you to tone the muscles of your back and strengthens the spine.

Technique:

- Lie face down. Relax all the muscles and be at ease. Place the palms on the

BHUJANGASANA

86

sides just below the shoulders. Breathe in and slowly raise the head, then the upper part of the body. Do not come up with a jerk. You have to come up little by little so that you actually feel the bending of each vertebra one by one. Curve the spine well. The navel must remain on the ground.

- Hold the breath in the position, then breathe out slowly while coming down. Repeat the process six times.

4. *Sinha asana* – is a posture that resembles a lion, about to attack. It tones up the muscles and nerves and improves circulation.

Technique:

- Kneel on the floor sitting on heels, feet parallel and almost together, with toes turned under (like a lion about to spring).

- Place your hands on your knees. Relax.

- Now, and all at the same time, with all the force you can bring to bear, extend or spread your fingers as far as they will go, open your eyes very wide, as far as they will open. Take a very deep breath. Thrust out your tongue with all your might.

- Tense up your arm and leg muscles, making them rigid. Hold this position for one minute. Do this exercise three times.

5. *Sukh asana* or easy posture is a comfortable sitting position. It is described by Lord Krishna in the Bhagavad Gita.

- To assume this position, sit on the floor with legs outstretched in front of you. Bend the right leg and place the left leg under the right thigh. Pull your toes back towards you. The knees should be as low to the floor as possible, but without discomfort, straining, or conscious effort.

- Sitting on a pillow may help. If you have difficulty getting into this position, do the best you can. Practice makes a man perfect.

- And remember, it should be comfortable, for it is a position you will use for breathing exercises and deep meditation. Sit up straight, with head erect and eyes closed. Place your wrists on your knees, palms up. Gently touch the thumb to the index fingers, opening the other fingers.

- Concentrate on relaxing, breathing, clearing the mind, and concentrating. Imagine you are staring at a point between the eyebrows or at the tip of your nose. At first this may cause some discomfort, but this will pass with practise.

6. *Shavasana* or the position of the corpse is
    the *asana* with which your exercise
    programme is concluded. It is one of the
    easiest to practise and helps you relax
    completely at the end of your yogic
    exercise.

Pranayam

The meaning of *pranayama* is explained thus: *prana* means life-force or energy, and *yama* means control of that energy. Some scholars interpret this as *ayama*, meaning expansion – in this case *pranayama* is extension or expansion of the flow of energy.

Prana also means primary energy – the life that animates the universe. Thus there is the indelible link between man and the universe, for the same life-force is manifest in both. Further, it is the breath which links the body and the mind. Hence its importance to mental, physical and spiritual well-being cannot be underestimated.

Pranayama is a unique, systematic deep breathing exercise, associated with yoga. *Pranayama*, when practised in the proper method, enables the lungs to absorb optimum levels of oxygen so as to purify the blood, and thus ease the strain on the heart. Deep breathing brings immense benefits to us, including a stable mind, steady thinking, inner peace and a long life.

Experts teach us that there are four stages of *Pranayam:*

1) Sit in the posture of Padmasana. Inhale deeply and slowly upto the count of 5. This stage is called *purakha*.

2) Now, hold your breath up to the count of 10. This is known as *antrank kumbhaka*.

3) Exhale gradually, counting up to 5. This is called *rechaka*.

4) When the exhalation is complete, hold the breath up to the count of 10.

Holding the breath may be difficult to practise at first. In that case, you may close both nostrils with the thumb and fingers. You can gradually increase the counting period, until you are comfortable.

Prana or breath is the vital energy of our lives. Indeed, our life depends on breath. If we practise *pranayam,* it is bound to have a positive effect on our body, by enhancing our energy and vitality levels. Oxygen supply to the lungs increases manifold, and our body and brain are energised.

Pranayam is also a vital accompaniment of *dhyan* or meditation. As wise men from the East and West have repeatedly told us, the mind is the root cause of many diseases and ailments. With the help of *pranayam* and meditation, we can attain the blessed gift of a healthy mind in a healthy body. Some scholars define *prana* not just as "breath" or "energy" but as the "vital current" in the body. They regard *prana* as the crucial link between absolute consciousness and the mind and body. However, they agree that there is intimate connection between *prana* and breath, and rhythmic breathing is always considered to be *pranayama.*

Some experts also say that *pranayama* can only be practised under the guidance of a competent guru. However, such are the tremendous benefits associated with rhythmic breathing, that thousands of people have taken to simplified forms of *pranayama* such as deep-breathing exercises. This is usually a combination of *purakha* (filling in), *rechaka* (emptying) and *kumbhaka* (holding). There are no negative effects associated with such exercises. They help you relax, and overcome stress.

Obstacles On The Path Of Yoga

Yoga is for everyone; it is not the monopoly of chosen few. The path of yoga is open to each and every one of us. For yoga, difficult and cumbersome postures are not needed. Even Kapila and Patanjali, the great exponents of yoga, tell us that all we need is to sit in an easy, comfortable, stable and relaxed posture. Only see to it that the head, the neck and the spine are in a straight line.

Many people labour under the impression that *pranayama* is a technique that is difficult to master. I remember a lovely incident in the life of my Beloved Master, Sadhu Vaswani. He was asked, "Do you practise *pranayama*?" His reply was significant indeed. He said, "My *pranayama* is *Rama Nama*."

Sri Aurobindo, who has written and talked about yoga, does not emphasise the technical aspects. He stresses instead, that the consciousness must be lifted to a higher level. Sri Raman Maharishi, the great sage of Thiruvannamalai, said to his disciples, "Why waste time on *asanas* and *pranayama*? Just lift up your consciousness!"

Our minds alas, are scattered. They are dispersed – because they are tainted with desire. We need to purify our minds. The level of our consciousness needs to be raised. The seat of the mind is between and a little behind the two eyebrows. But the mind is looking downwards. We need to turn the gaze of the mind upwards. Therefore it is, that seemingly out of nowhere, impure thoughts wake up within our hearts.

We must be on our guard against three things that make our minds impure. They are the three obstacles on the path of yoga.

The very first obstacle is love of pleasure; the desire for sense-gratification and sense-indulgence. Sri Ramakrishna referred to this obstacle as "*kamini*" – one whom we must guard against.

There is a fable about the bee, which found a pot of honey left near the hive. The bee thought to itself, "Now why should I labour all day, flying from flower to flower, gathering honey little by little? Here is a store of honey which I can reach easily – and it's all mine!"

So the bee went into the pot and revelled in the honey. When it began to get tired and cloyed, the poor bee found that its wings and feet were clogged – and it could not drag itself out of the sticky mess of honey. The bee died and got buried in its own pleasure!

We are told that the Devil once called a meeting of all his associates. The forces of evil were all present at the meeting – each one boasting of his victories and conquests. Anger, envy, greed and jealously were all boasting of their numerous victims. Soon a heated argument ensued: who, among them, could take the credit for wreaking the greatest havoc on mankind?

Impurity won, hands down. Conferring the dubious distinction upon him, the Devil himself remarked: "He is the one with the sharpest sword, the deadliest poison. All he has to do is to sow a single thought of impurity in the mind – it is enough to cause the greatest havoc."

I am reminded of my Beloved Master Sadhu Vaswani. When he was a student, he carried a pin with him. Whenever an angry or negative thought entered his mind, he would prick himself with the pin, so that the impure thought could be thrown out at once.

Following his example, I too developed the habit of stopping every impure thought in its tracks. I would slap myself sharply, when such a thought intervened.

"Was that a mosquito?" my friends would ask me. "Yes – the deadliest," I would reply. For an impure thought is the deadliest and most infectious bite!

The second obstacle on the path of yoga is greed of gold – the desire to amass wealth.

We all know the story of King Midas – he whose greed for gold was legendary. He obtained a boon from the Gods, so that all that he touched would be turned into gold. He had a wonderful time to begin with! He touched everything around him and it turned to gold. His joy knew no bounds. Within a day, he was surrounded by as much gold as a man could ever wish for.

Tired and famished, he asked for a meal to be brought to him. No sooner did he lay his hands on the food, than it turned to gold. Bread, fruits, vegetables, whatever he touched, turned to gold. Which was all very well – but what could he eat? Gold could satisfy his greed – but it could not appease his hunger!

A sadder, wiser Midas offered to return his boon to the Gods – for he had learnt that gold could not bring him all that a man needed.

The third prong of *maya*, which hinders us on the path of yoga is desire for power – desire for fame, name, publicity, popularity and earthly greatness.

How low a man sometimes stoops to gain power, position and authority! We would have no graft or corruption in the world today, were it not for such men. And then there is flattery, falsehood and hypocrisy which people adopt to please those in power. Such practices only point to the lowest self in man. These undesirable elements only taint our minds and hearts and impede our spiritual progress – which is the only progress that matters.

What is it that we seek through this power and glory? Where will they lead us eventually? To what avail is earthly greatness when we know that anytime the call can come for us – and we shall all be reduced to nothing more than a handful of dust and ashes!

To defend ourselves against the three pronged attack of *maya*, we need faith and willpower. For this, we must pray, again and again, to the Lord. In the Gita is unfolded a memorable picture of a tortoise. Once the tortoise draws in its limbs, you will not be able to draw them out, even if you cut the creature into four pieces. This is the kind of willpower we need to develop if we would wish to tread the path of yoga. Patanjali also lists nine *antarayas* or obstacles which we encounter on the path of yoga: he describes them as rocks which obstruct the path of the aspirant. These are:

1) Illness
2) Lethargy
3) Doubt
4) Haste or impatience

5) Fatigue

6) Distraction

7) Arrogance

8) Inability to proceed

9) Loss of confidence

These are manifested as physical symptoms as well as in a negative attitude to life.

1. Illness: Physical Illness disturbs mind and body. One cannot undertake yogic practices in a state of ill-health.

2. Lethargy: Our mood has a direct bearing on our minds. When we feel low and lethargic, we are under the influence of *tamas,* and we cannot do anything useful. This condition can be caused by overeating, eating the wrong kind of food or by cold weather.

3. Doubt or *samsaya* is a negative and persistent feeling which creates uncertainty

in the mind. This can severely undermine our practice of yoga.

4. Haste, leading to impatience and rashness will cause us to slip instead of making progress.

5. Fatigue or exhaustion, known as *alasya* leads to negative thinking. Our confidence is undermined, and our energy is depleted. At such a stage we need to be remotivated to pursue our yogic practices.

6. Distraction or *avirati* impedes our concentration and leads us to temptation. We are led in the wrong direction and lose our concentration on yoga.

7. Arrogance is perhaps the greatest hurdle we must overcome. When we think we know everything, we lose ourselves in *avidya* – ignorance and illusion.

8. Inability to proceed – to take the next step- causes us to become disheartened. We feel

that our goal is still too far, and we are inclined to give up our pursuit.

9. Loss of confidence makes us feel that we can neither maintain the position we reached, nor progress further on the path. As a result we fall back, losing whatever we have gained.

These are the obstacles we may encounter on the path of yoga. A good teacher can help us overcome these setbacks, and put us on the right track once again. Even more effective is submission to the Lord's Will – *ishwarapranidhara*. God is the highest Spiritual Being – and surrendering to His Will, can only bring us the benefits of His blessing.

The True Yogi

It has been my privilege, my good fortune, to have come in contact with a true yogi, Sadhu Vaswani – to have lived at his Lotus Feet for several years, to have been blessed by his holy hands, to have listened to the pearls of wisdom that dropped out of his gentle lips.

One day, I asked him, "Who is a true yogi?"

He said, "The true yogi is even he who beholds the Lord in the Lotus of his heart."

A stage comes in the life of every aspirant, in the life of every true yogi, when he sees God face-to-face. He touches God; he talks to God; he experiences God. He has a vision of God in the lotus of his heart. Then, as he opens his eyes, he finds the face of God shining in everyone around him. He finds the one face of God in all men; yea, in all birds and animals, in every tree, every shrub, every plant, every blade of grass. Having had this trem ndous experience, he exclaims:

Jidhar dekhta hoon udhar Tu hi Tu hai!
Ke har shai mein jalwa Tera Hubahu hai!

A true yogi feels the thrill of the presence of God in everyone around him. At the same time, he makes another discovery, that though God dwells within every man, men know it not. And therefore, they are unhappy. Every true yogi says to himself: I shall be a servant of suffering humanity. I shall serve those that suffer and are in pain. Verily, true yoga flowers into action; it flowers into the noblest service.

Concerning one such yogi I read many years ago. He was the only son of a rich businessman. His father, a rich merchant, suddenly passed away and the son said to himself: "My father has moved on leaving all the wealth behind – this wealth was of no use to him. He could not carry one single *paisa* with himself. Of what use will all this wealth be to me?" And so he distributes all his wealth to the poor and retires to the solitude of the Himalayan heights. There he goes and lives a life of meditation. He meditates from more to more. He sinks deeper and deeper within himself, until one blessed day in the lotus of the heart within, he beholds the shining Face of God. He meets God face-to-face. And then as he opens his eyes, he finds the one Face of God, the one divine Face in everything, in everyone around him. God in the mountains, God in the stone, God in the tree, God in the shrub, God in the plant. God in the animal, God in every man, God in every grain of sand, God in every drop of water. God in every ray of sunshine. And he begins to exclaim:

Jidhar dekhta hoon udhar Tu hi Tu hai!
Ke har shai mein jalwa Tera Hubahu hai!
Wherever I turn, I behold Thee, Lord!
In everything I see, I perceive Thy splendour.

This is the experience of every true yogi.

And now he descends from the mountain heights. He comes to the planes below. He goes to the villages, where dwell the poor and broken ones. He takes with himself medicinal herbs. He moves on from one cottage to another distributing medicinal herbs to the poor and the sick. He meets them in love. He speaks to them. He looks into their needs. He shows them the right way to true happiness, true *ananda*. And every day in the morning and in the evening he goes and sits underneath a tree to meditate.

One day as he is sitting under the tree in meditation, the King of Banaras, proud of his power, intoxicated with drink, happens to pass by. The king sees this yogi sitting underneath a tree. He comes near the yogi and says to him: "O you who sit with closed eyes, tell me what is it that you teach?" The yogi does not open his eyes, and the king feels offended. He unsheathes his sword and holding it in his hands says: "If you will not open your eyes, if you will not give me an answer, I shall kill you."

Then it is that the yogi opens his eyes. And looking quietly, gently, lovingly into the face of the king says to him: "O king, you cannot kill me for I am deathless. I am immortal. I am immutable. I am eternal. You can but destroy this body." The king is amazed at the fearlessness of this yogi. And he feels ashamed of his conduct. He looks into the eyes of the yogi and finds that they are lit up with a strange, mystic light. He falls down at the feet of the yogi and begs for forgiveness. And he says to the yogi: "O yogi, do kindly tell me, what is it that you teach?" And the yogi says to him: "O king, this is what I teach. Cleanse your heart. Be humble. And give the service of love to all who suffer and are in pain."

In these few simple words is given to us the very essence of the message of yoga. In these few simple words is given to us the very secret of the life of yoga: "Cleanse your heart, be humble and give the service of love to those who suffer and are in pain."

The Science of Yoga Mudra

The science of Yoga *Mudra* is an important part of yoga. *Mudras* are special signs or positions of the fingers of the hand, used in yoga, ritual worship as well as in ancient dance forms.

It is believed that a special form of electro-magnetic energy from our bodies is emitted through our hands and fingers. It is this energy that is used by experts in Touch Therapy and Accupressure, to treat some ailments.

There is also the belief that the five basic elements which go to make up our bodies (earth, water, fire, air and space) are represented by the five fingers on each hand. Thus it was that ancient *rishis* believed that by touching our hands or folding fingers in a particular way, or pressing certain points on the palms, we could release the healing energies of our body.

1. *Mudras* can be practised by all – men, women and children.

2. No strict rules of posture are necessary for performing *mudras*. We can perform them even while we are watching television or travelling or walking.

3. *Mudras* are performed with both hands. Right-handed *mudras* influence the left side of our body and vice versa.

4. One should begin by practising *mudras* for 10 to 15 minutes regularly in the morning and evening. This should lead up to a session of at least 45 minutes a day, if we wish to see a beneficial effect on the body.

5. *Mudra* therapy can be undertaken along with any other treatment.

Whether one is ailing or healthy, *mudras* can be practised for balance, harmony and well-being.

A few important *mudras* are:

1. *Gyana Mudra*:

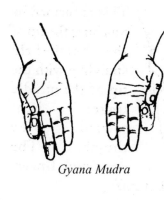

Gyana Mudra

This is formed by touching the tip of the thumb with the tip of the index finger – gently, without pressing, the remaining fingers are kept straight, without stiffness.

This *mudra* increases brain-power; it releases tension and helps you overcome emotional disorders like anger, depression and over-excitement. It also increases the power of concentration. It is therefore, especially useful for students and small children. *Gyana mudra* is also used in the treatment of mental disorders, and as an effective cure for insomnia.

2. *Akash Mudra*:

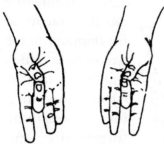

Akash Mudra

This is formed by touching the tip of the thumb—held straight – with the tip of the middle finger – bent towards the thumb. The remaining fingers are kept straight, but not stiff.

This *mudra* increases the *akash* or space element in our body. It is especially useful to the heart, which is directly linked with the middle finger. The thumb and middle finger are used also during the chanting of beads.

3. *Prithvi Mudra*:

This is formed when the ring finger and thumb come together.

This *mudra* helps to maintain the earth element in our body, and removes all physical

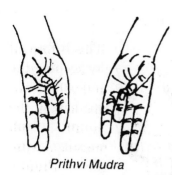

Prithvi Mudra

weakness. It is used by people who wish to increase their weight. It also increases the lustre of the skin. It makes the mind happy and generous.

4. *Varun Mudra*:

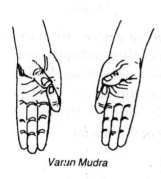

Varun Mudra

This is formed by bringing the tips of the thumb and little finger together.

It balances the water elements in our body and helps restore moisture to dry skin. It also helps to remove impurities in the blood, and relieves cramps.

115

5. *Vayu Mudra*:

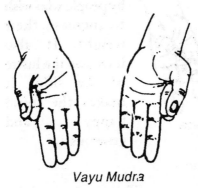

Vayu Mudra

This is formed by keeping the index finger at the base of the thumb and pressing it with the thumb against the Mount of Venus.

This decreases the level of *vayu* or air in the body. It also cures rheumatism, arthritis, gout, etc, if practised intensely and continually. It is also used in the treatment of cervical spondylitis. People with knee-pain derive great relief from the practice of this *mudra*.

6. *Prana Mudra*:

This is formed by bending the little finger and ring finger so that their tips touch the front-

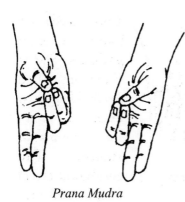

Prana Mudra

edge (tip) of the thumb. The remaining two fingers are kept straight.

This is an important *mudra* which increases our vitality, strengthening us mentally and physically. It is said to improve circulation and clear blocks in blood vessels. It also raises our immunity against diseases, strengthens weak muscles and improves eyesight.

7. *Apan Vayu Mudra*:

The index finger touches the base of the thumb; and the tip of the thumb touches the tip of the middle finger and ring finger. The little finger remains straight.

This *mudra* is a boon for heart patients, and is therefore called *hriday-mudra* or even *mrit-sanjeevani mudra*. The combined effect of *apan* and *vayu*

Apan Vayu Mudra

cures diseases like stomach disorders, gastric diseases and regularizes bowel movements.

This *mudra* has been practised regularly by thousands of heart patients with extremely beneficial effects.

8. *Dhyana Mudra*:

This *mudra* is formed by sitting in *padmasana* and keeping right palm tightly on the left palm.

During this *mudra*, the head, neck and back should be kept erect. Eyes and lips are closed.

118

Dhyana Mudra

The *sadhak* focuses on his *ishtadevta* until he attains peace.

This is the most important *mudra* for self-realisation. It is performed in *ashtanga* yoga during meditation. It gives mental rest and peace; it increases pious and devout thoughts in the mind of the practitioner and enables him to attain self-realisation.

Glossary

Words	Meaning
Abhyasi	Practitioner
Ahimsa	Abstinence from injury to any living creature through thought, word or deed, non-violence
Ajna	Literally, "the command center." It is a center of consciousness located between the eyebrows
Alasya	Lethargy
Anahata	Literally, "the unstruck center." This center of consciousness corresponds to the physical cardiac plexus located in the hollow just beneath the breast bone in the middle of the chest

Ananda	Bliss, absolute joy
Antahakarna	The inner instrument of the mind
Antarayas	Obstacles
Aparigraha	Non-possession, desire-lessness, the state in which one is free from craving
Asana	Yogic posture
Ashtanga Yoga	The Yoga of eight limbs or steps
Asteya	Non-stealing
Atman	The real immortal self
Avidya	Ignorance, Misconception
Avirati	Distraction
Ayama	Expansion
Ayurveda	Science of life, an ancient established system of therapy

Bhaktas	An adherent of the yogic path who aspires to God-realization through love and surrender to God
Brahmacharya	Chastity, continence in thought, word and deed
Dhyana	To think repeatedly, meditation
Ekagrita	Single-mindedness
Ishwarapranidhara	To surrender and offer all actions to God without attachment to the fruits of our actions
Jignasu	A seeker, an aspirant
Karma	Mental or physical action
Kriyas	Deed, Operation, effort
Kundalini	Serpent power, it is the spiritual energy lying dormant in all individuals

Mahakavya	A great work of literature
Maharishi	A Great seer
Manipura	Literally, the "jeweled city." The center of consciousness which corresponds to the solar plexus located in the navel area
Mantra	Name of God or of an Avatar or Ishtadev
Maya	Deception, illusion, appearance
Mudras	Special signs or positions of the fingers of the hand
Mukti	Moksha, liberation
Muladhara	Literally, the "fundament" or the "root-support center," it corresponds to the sacral, or pelvic, nerve plexus at the base of the physical spine

Niyama	Prescribed duties
Padmasan	Lotus position
Prana	Life-force or energy
Pranayama	Yogic breathing exercise, control and regulation of breath
Pratihara	Restraint of the senses from sense-enjoyment
Ramayana	The life story of Rama; the oldest epic in Sanskrit literature
Rishi	A sage, a seer or holy one
Sadhak	Seeker, aspirant, yoga practitioner
Sadhana	Correct sustained practice that leads to accomplishment
Samadhi	Union, completion

Samatwa	Equanimity
Samsaya	Doubt
Sangha	A group of seekers who gather around a Master or Guru in order to attain spiritual knowledge and realisation of the highest truth
Sansar sagara	The ocean of life
Satsang	The company or intercourse with holy people or conscientious seekers of God
Satya	Truthfulness
Shakti	Power, force, energy
Shishu	A child of God
Shishya	Disciple
Siddhi	Accomplishments, supernatural powers, one of the results of yogic practice

Surya Namaskar	Sequence of *asanas* collectively called the salute to the Sun
Sutras	A thread - a brief aphorism used by Indian philosophers to present a subject in a cogent way
Swadisthana	The center of consciousness, "her own abode," corresponding to the plexus located just above the genital area
Tapobana	A forest of meditation
Tattva Darshana	Someone who has beheld and understood the secret of life
Vaikunth	Vishnu's paradise, variously described as on Mount Meru

Vishuddha	Literally, "purified." This center corresponds to the level of the base, along the spinal column
Yama	Moral restrains, don'ts for a Yogi
Yogeswara	Lord of yoga, name attributed to Lord Krishna and Lord Shiva
Yug	To unite

Dada J.P. Vaswani needs no introduction to readers of inspirational literature. He is regarded as one of the leading spiritual luminaries of India, a practical philosopher and man of God whose grace has reached and influenced thousands of people all over the world.

A gifted writer and brilliant orator, Dada J.P. Vaswani has been the recipient of several honours, including the prestigious U Thant Peace Award. He has written over 80 books which have been translated into several Indian and foreign languages.